Math All Around

Sorting at the Ocean

Jennifer Rozines Roy and Gregory Roy

 Marshall Cavendish
Benchmark
New York

Come to the seashore and look out at the **ocean**. Below the rolling white waves live thousands of kinds of animals and plants in different colors, shapes, and sizes.

How can we learn and understand more about things that seem so different from one another? By sorting!

When you sort things, you put them in groups with other objects that are like them.

Let's put on our diving gear, dive into the ocean, and sort things out!

3

Wow! See the fish swimming among the plants and the sea animals moving from one place to another?

We can make sense of what we see by sorting them into sets. A **set** is a group of objects that are alike.

First, let's make a set of the fish.

Fish

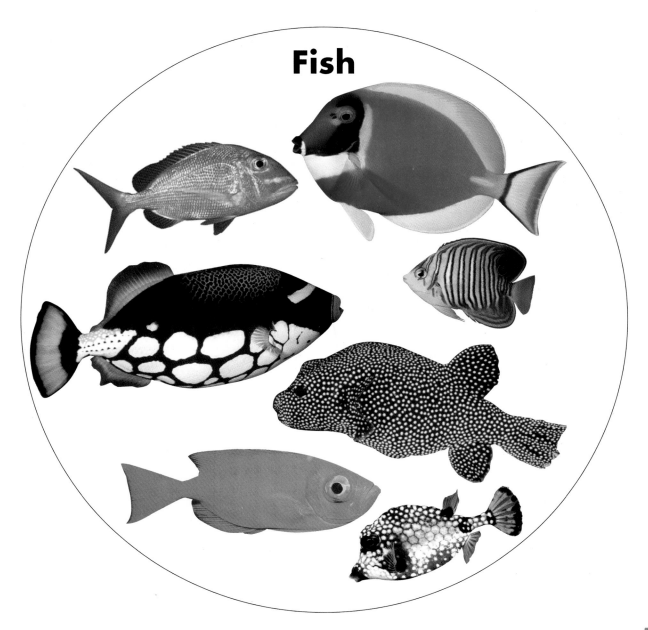

So many beautiful and unusual creatures live in the sea. These sea animals can be placed in our second set of sea creatures. They are *not* fish.

Sea Animals

Towers and bunches of **seaweed** provide homes and food to ocean wildlife. Let's put them in our last set.

Seaweed

Swim up to the fish for a closer look. Let them swim around you.

We can sort our set of fish by color, by shape, or by size.

Color

Shape

Size

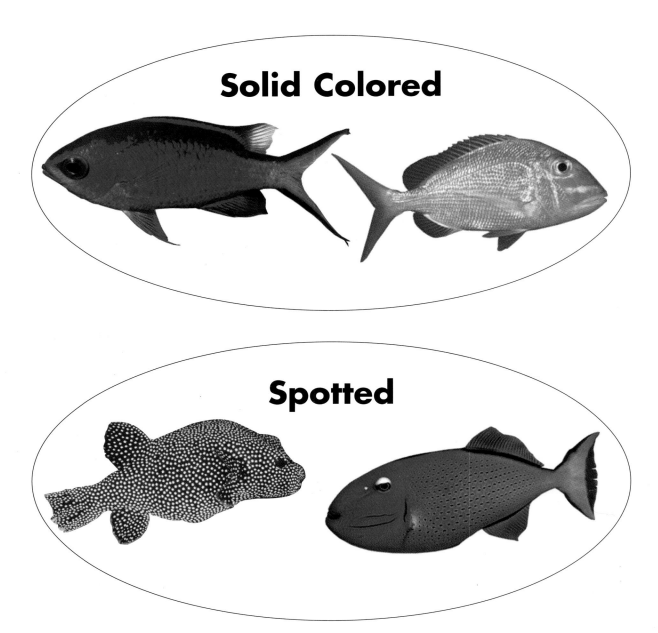

Solid Colored

Spotted

Fish come in different patterns, too. We can sort them into sets of solid colored, spotted, and striped fish.

Striped

Oops! You almost got bumped by a sea turtle.
He seemed friendly, but his hard shell could hurt.
Let's sort our set of sea animals into two
smaller sets.

Sea Animals with Shells

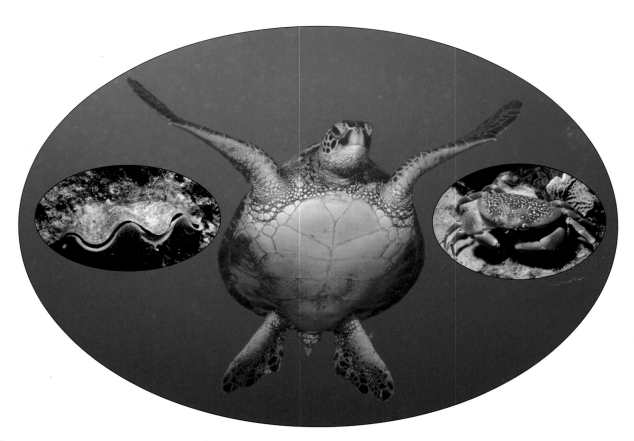

Sea Animals without Shells

In the ocean, some sets of animals have special names. A set of whales is a pod. A set of fish that belong to the same family is called a school.

This school of snappers has sorted itself into a tight group, so it makes it harder for them to get eaten by a bigger creature!

Sharks! Let's swim back toward the shore to be safe. Sharks are not always dangerous, but their sharp teeth sure make them look scary.

Look at this shark. It is different from the rest of the set. The hammerhead shark, with its hammer-shaped snout, can be called the "odd one out."

Heading back to shore, we pass some mussels on a rock. We also spot a starfish and a sea urchin. Just don't get too close to the octopus!

Starfish

Octopus

These creatures can be sorted into two categories. A **category** is the name of a group of things that are alike.

The mussel and the octopus belong to the mollusk family. This category is called mollusks.

Mollusks

Mussels

Starfish and sea urchins are echinoderms. They go in the "echinoderm" category.

Echinoderms

Sea Urchins

The water is getting shallow. There are many rocks on the sea floor here. Let's sort them using a **Venn diagram**. A Venn diagram uses circles to compare and contrast things.

The dark-colored rocks are in the first circle. All of the rocks in the second circle are round. The ones in the middle are round and dark. They belong in both sets.

Time to come up for air! Our adventure is about to end.

Do you see what is floating on the water's surface? Garbage. Sadly, some people dump trash into the sea.

Paper, glass, and plastic are in this mess. Let's gather them, sort them, and put them into bags. Then they can be **recycled**.

Our journey under the sea is done, but wasn't it "sort" of fun? Sorting helped us to learn about the ocean, and it can help you understand how things in the world are alike and how they are different.

How do you use sorting in *your* life?

Glossary

category—A group that shows how objects in a set are alike.

ocean—The body of salt water that covers much of the Earth's surface.

recycle—To use something over and over again or to make ready to reuse.

seaweed—Plants that live in the ocean.

set—A group of things that are alike.

Venn diagram—A way of sorting that uses a circle or circles to show groups.

Read More

Johnson, Jinney. *Children's Guide to Sea Creatures*. New York: Simon & Schuster, 1998.

Kirkby, David. *Sorting*. Crystal Lake, IL: Rigby Education, 1996.

Patilla, Peter. *Sorting*. Des Plaines, IL: Heinemann Library, 2000.

Plucrose, Henry. *Sorting and Sets*. Milwaukee, WI: Gareth Stevens Publishing, 2001.

Web Sites

A+ Math
www.aplusmath.com

Cool Math 4 Kids
www.coolmath4kids.com

The Math Forum: Ask Dr. Math
http://mathforum.org/dr.math

Index

Page numbers in **boldface** are illustrations.

About the Authors

Jennifer Rozines Roy is the author of more than twenty books. A former Gifted and Talented teacher, she holds degrees in psychology and elementary education.

Gregory Roy is a civil engineer who has co-authored several books with his wife. The Roys live in upstate New York with their son Adam.

Marshall Cavendish Benchmark
99 White Plains Road
Tarrytown, New York 10591-9001
www.marshallcavendish.us

Library of Congress Cataloging-in-Publication Data

Roy, Jennifer Rozines, 1967-
Sorting at the ocean / by Jennifer Rozines Roy and Gregory Roy.
p. cm. — (Math all around)
Summary: "Reinforces both sorting and reading skills, stimulates critical thinking,
and provides students with an understanding of math in the real world"—Provided by publisher.
Includes bibliographical references and index.
ISBN 0-7614-1998-5
1. Set theory—Juvenile literature. I. Roy, Gregory. II. Title. III. Series.
QA248.R69 2005
511.3'22—dc22
2005003514

Photo Research by Anne Burns Images

Cover Photo by *Corbis/*Brandon D. Cole

The photographs in this book are used with permission and through the courtesy of:
Photo Researchers: pp. 1, 15 Fred McConnaughey; pp. 5 crb, 10 bl Rudiger Lehnen; p. 5 bl Andrew G. Wood; pp. 5 br, 7 (l inset)
Andrew Martinez; p.7 (background) Jeff Rotman; p. 8 (both) Mark Smith; p. 10 tl Charles V. Angelo; p. 16 Alexis Rosenfeld;
p. 20 Michael Lustbader. *Peter Arnold*: p. 2 Tom Vezo; pp. 5 tl, 6 tr, 10 tr, 12 r Fred Bavendam; pp. 5 tr, 9 tl, 9 bl, 10 br,
11 l Secret Sea Visions; pp. 5 cl & ctr, 9 br Rudolf Schnorrenberg; pp. 6 tl, 13 t KLEIN; pp. 6 bl & br, 12 c Carl Miller; pp. 6 bc,
12 l Jeffrey L.Rotman; pp. 9 tr, 11 r, 13 (inset) Kelvin Aitken; p. 14 Douglas Seifert; p. 17 Doug Perrine; pp. 18, 21 l Ed Reschke;
pp. 19, 20 (inset) Norbert Wu; p. 21 r Bob Evans; p. 24 A. & F. Michler; p. 25 Ray Pfortner. *Corbis*: p. 4 Larry Williams;
p. 7 (r inset) Hal Beral; p. 23 l Bill Miles; p. 23 c Michael T. Sedam; p. 23 r Paul Edmondson; p. 27 Jim Sugar.

Series design by Virginia Pope

Printed in Malaysia
1   3   5   6   4   2